The Brothers Grimm Interactive Reader

High School Book 1

The Golden Bird and *Hans in Luck* are stories from the Brothers Grimm collections and are in the public domain. All other work © LW. All rights reserved. Permission to copy restricted without permission from publisher. 2014.

ISBN-13: 978-0692407288 (Lucky Willy Publishing)
ISBN-10: 0692407286

Table of Contents

The Golden Bird — **page 5**
    Theme CCSS 9-10 RL.2 — page 11
    Character Analysis CCSS 9-10 RL.3 — page 12
    Author's Choice n Text Structuring CCSS 9-10 RL.4/5 — page 13
    Digging Deeper: Critical Thinking for 21st Century — page 14
    Summary Writing CCSS 9-10 W.4/5 — page 15

PBL: Multimedia Project — **page 16**

Who Were the Grimm Brothers? Information Text (RI.2) — **page 17**

Hans in Luck — **page 18**
    Literary Devices CCSS 9-10 RL.6 — page 23
    Multi-Media Comparison CCSS 9-10 RL.7 — page 25
    Writing Arguments CCSS 9-10 W.1 — page 26

Non-Fiction: Around the World 1812ish CCSS 9-10 RI.2/7 — **page 27**
    PBL CCSS.W1 and W.7 and RH.2 and RH.3

Appendix — **page 29**
    Writing Rubric — page 30
    Critical Response Rubric — page 31

References — **page 32**

Notes:

This workbook is designed to cover one-quarter of the Common Core State Standards in English for the 9 and 10th grades. The writing requirements should be used to teach and emphasize all of the Common Core State Standards for Language - as proper grammar usage must be relevant and applicable to real world settings. Reading and Writing Standards specifically addressed in this first of four parts include:

> CCSS 9-10 RL.2
> CCSS 9-10 RL.3
> CCSS 9-10 RL.4
> CCSS 9-10 RL.5
> CCSS 9-10 RL.6
> CCSS 9-10 RL.7
>
> CCSS 9-10 RI.2
> CCSS 9-10 RI.3
> CCSS 9-10 RI.7
>
> CCSS 9-10 W.1
> CCSS 9-10 W.4
> CCSS 9-10 W.5
> CCSS 9-10 W.7
>
> CCSS 9-10 RH.2
> CCSS 9-10 RH.3

The Common Core State Standards strands and what they mean:

Reading Literature: This strand encompasses literary fiction. Texts read at this grade level including: stories, novels, drama and poetry. The Common Core State Standards stress that all students should read a variety and range of texts, of increasing complexity, as they progresses from grade to grade.

Reading Informational Text: Informational Text includes a range of non-fictional writing such as exposition, functional and informaion. Genres include essays, speeches, opinion pieces and memoirs as well as scientific and historical writing.

Writing: The Writing strand, at this level, focuses on three types of work – informative, arguments and narratives. This strand includes using the writing process and technology to research, develop and publish ideas. The Common Core State Standards emphasize research as well as both long and short writing exercises.

Language: The Common Core State Standards for the language strand encompass conventions of standard English grammar, mechanics, knowledge of language, and vocabulary use and acquisition.

The Golden Bird

A certain king had a beautiful garden, and in the garden stood a tree which bore golden apples. These apples were always counted, and about the time when they began to grow ripe it was found that every night one of them was gone. The king became very angry at this, and ordered the gardener to keep watch all night under the tree. The gardener set his eldest son to watch; but about twelve o'clock he fell asleep, and in the morning another of the apples was missing. Then the second son was ordered to watch; and at midnight he too fell asleep, and in the morning another apple was gone. Then the third son offered to keep watch; but the gardener at first would not let him, for fear some harm should come to him: however, at last he consented, and the young man laid himself under the tree to watch. As the clock struck twelve he heard a rustling noise in the air, and a bird came flying that was of pure gold; and as it was snapping at one of the apples with its beak, the gardener's son jumped up and shot an arrow at it. But the arrow did the bird no harm; only it dropped a golden feather from its tail, and then flew away. The golden feather was brought to the king in the morning, and all the council was called together. Everyone agreed that it was worth more than all the wealth of the kingdom: but the king said, 'One feather is of no use to me, I must have the whole bird.'

Then the gardener's eldest son set out and thought to find the golden bird very easily; and when he had gone but a little way, he came to a wood, and by the side of the wood he saw a fox sitting; so he took his bow

---

Active Reading: What is the significance of the apples?

_____
_____
_____
_____
_____
_____
_____

CCSS RL. 1
What does the text on this page say?

_____
_____
_____
_____
_____
_____
_____

What can I infer from what is said?

_____
_____
_____
_____
_____
_____
_____
_____

CCSS.R.2 Theme

What theme is emerging in this story?

_____
_____
_____
_____
_____
_____
_____
_____
_____

Explain what is happening to support the emergence of this theme?

_____
_____
_____
_____
_____
_____
_____
_____
_____

Circle the most important sentence(s) on this page.

and made ready to shoot at it. Then the fox said, 'Do not shoot me, for I will give you good counsel; I know what your business is, and that you want to find the golden bird. You will reach a village in the evening; and when you get there, you will see two inns opposite to each other, one of which is very pleasant and beautiful to look at: go not in there, but rest for the night in the other, though it may appear to you to be very poor and mean.' But the son thought to himself, 'What can such a beast as this know about the matter?' So he shot his arrow at the fox; but he missed it, and it set up its tail above its back and ran into the wood. Then he went his way, and in the evening came to the village where the two inns were; and in one of these were people singing, and dancing, and feasting; but the other looked very dirty, and poor. 'I should be very silly,' said he, 'if I went to that shabby house, and left this charming place'; so he went into the smart house, and ate and drank at his ease, and forgot the bird, and his country too.

Time passed on; and as the eldest son did not come back, and no tidings were heard of him, the second son set out, and the same thing happened to him. He met the fox, who gave him the good advice: but when he came to the two inns, his eldest brother was standing at the window where the merrymaking was, and called to him to come in; and he could not withstand the temptation, but went in, and forgot the golden bird and his country in the same manner.

Time passed on again, and the youngest son too wished to set out into the wide world to seek for the golden bird; but his father would not listen to it for a long while, for he was very fond of his son, and was afraid that some ill

6

luck might happen to him also, and prevent his coming back. However, at last it was agreed he should go, for he would not rest at home; and as he came to the wood, he met the fox, and heard the same good counsel. But he was thankful to the fox, and did not attempt his life as his brothers had done; so the fox said, 'Sit upon my tail, and you will travel faster.' So he sat down, and the fox began to run, and away they went over stock and stone so quick that their hair whistled in the wind.

When they came to the village, the son followed the fox's counsel, and without looking about him went to the shabby inn and rested there all night at his ease. In the morning came the fox again and met him as he was beginning his journey, and said, 'Go straight forward, till you come

Illustrate the story so far:

to a castle, before which lie a whole troop of soldiers fast asleep and snoring: take no notice of them, but go into the castle and pass on and on till you come to a room, where the golden bird sits in a wooden cage; close by it stands a beautiful golden cage; but do not try to take the bird out of the shabby cage and put it into the handsome one, otherwise you will repent it.' Then the fox stretched out his tail again, and the young man sat himself down, and away they went over stock and stone till their hair whistled in the wind.

Before the castle gate all was as the fox had said: so the son went in and found the chamber where the golden bird hung in a wooden cage, and below stood the golden cage, and the three golden apples that had been lost were lying close by it. Then thought he to himself, 'It will be a very droll thing to bring away such a fine bird in this shabby cage'; so he opened the door and took hold of it and put it into the golden cage. But the bird set up such a loud scream that all the soldiers awoke, and they took him prisoner and carried him before the king. The next morning the court sat to judge him; and when all was heard, it sentenced him to die, unless he should bring the king the golden horse which could run as swiftly as the wind; and if he did this, he was to have the golden bird given him for his own.

So he set out once more on his journey, sighing, and in great despair, when on a sudden his friend the fox met him, and said, 'You see now what has happened on account of your not listening to my counsel. I will still, however, tell you how to find the golden horse, if you will do as I bid you. You must go straight on till you come to the castle where the horse stands in his stall: by his side will lie the groom fast asleep and snoring: take away the horse quietly, but be sure to put the old leathern saddle upon him, and not the golden one that is close by it.' Then the son sat down on the fox's tail, and away they went over stock and stone till their hair whistled in the wind.

All went right, and the groom lay snoring with his hand upon the golden saddle. But when the son looked at the horse, he thought it a great pity to put the leathern saddle upon it. 'I will give him the good one,' said he; 'I am sure he deserves it.' As he took up the golden saddle the groom awoke and cried out so loud, that all the guards ran in and took him prisoner, and in the morning he was again brought before the court to be judged, and was sentenced to die. But it was agreed, that, if he could bring thither the beautiful princess, he should live, and have the bird and the horse given him for his own.

Then he went his way very sorrowful; but the old fox came and said, 'Why did not you listen to me? If you had, you would have carried away both the bird and the horse; yet will I once more give you counsel. Go straight on, and in the evening you will arrive at a castle. At twelve o'clock at night the princess goes to the bathing-house: go up to her and give her a kiss, and she will let you lead her away; but take care you do not suffer her to go and take leave of her father and mother.' Then the fox stretched out his tail, and so away they went over stock and stone till their hair whistled again.

As they came to the castle, all was as the fox had said, and at twelve o'clock the young man met the princess going to the bath and gave her the kiss, and she agreed to run away with him, but begged with many tears that he would let her take leave of her father. At first he refused, but she wept still more and more, and fell at his feet, till at last he consented; but the moment she came to her father's house the guards awoke and he was taken prisoner again.

Then he was brought before the king, and the king said, 'You shall never have my daughter unless in eight days you dig away the hill that stops the view from my window.' Now this hill was so big that the whole world could not take it away: and when he had worked for seven days, and had done very little, the fox came and said. 'Lie down and go to sleep; I will work for you.' And in the morning he awoke and the hill was gone; so he went merrily to the king, and told him that now that it was removed he must give him the princess.

Then the king was obliged to keep his word, and away went the young man and the princess; and the fox came and said to him, 'We will have all three, the princess, the horse, and the bird.' 'Ah!' said the young man, 'that would be a great thing, but how can you contrive it?'

'If you will only listen,' said the fox, 'it can be done. When you come to the king, and he asks for the beautiful princess, you must say, "Here she is!" Then he will be very joyful; and you will mount the golden horse that they are to give you, and put out your hand to take leave of them; but shake hands with the princess last. Then lift her quickly on to the horse behind you; clap your spurs to his side, and gallop away as fast as you can.'

All went right: then the fox said, 'When you come to the castle where the bird is, I will stay with the princess at the door, and you will ride in and speak to the king; and when he sees that it is the right horse, he will bring out the bird; but you must sit still, and say that you want to look at it, to see whether it is the true golden bird; and when you get it into your hand, ride away.'

This, too, happened as the fox said; they carried off the bird, the princess mounted again, and they rode on to a great wood. Then the fox came, and said, 'Pray kill me, and cut off my head and my feet.' But the young man refused to do it: so the fox said, 'I will at any rate give you good counsel: beware of two things; ransom no one from the gallows, and sit down by the side of no river.' Then away he went. 'Well,' thought the young man, 'it is no hard matter to keep that advice.'

He rode on with the princess, till at last he came to the village where he had left his two brothers. And there he heard a great noise and uproar; and when he asked what was the matter, the people said, 'Two men are going to be hanged.' As he came nearer, he saw that the two men were his brothers, who had turned robbers; so he said, 'Cannot they in any way be saved?' But the people said 'No,' unless he would bestow all his money upon the rascals and buy their liberty. Then he did not stay to think about the matter, but paid what was asked, and his brothers were given up, and went on with him towards their home.

Active Reading: Highlight the words that contribute to the mood of the story.

Write the most important ones here:
_____
_____
_____
_____
_____
_____
_____
_____
_____
_____
_____
_____
_____

And as they came to the wood where the fox first met them, it was so cool and pleasant that the two brothers said, 'Let us sit down by the side of the river, and rest a while, to eat and drink.' So he said, 'Yes,' and forgot the fox's counsel, and sat down on the side of the river; and while he suspected nothing, they came behind, and threw him down the bank, and took the princess, the horse, and the bird, and went home to the king their master, and said. 'All this have we won by our labour.' Then there was great rejoicing made; but the horse would not eat, the bird would not sing, and the princess wept.

The youngest son fell to the bottom of the river's bed: luckily it was nearly dry, but his bones were almost broken, and the bank was so steep that he could find no way to get out. Then the old fox came once more, and scolded him for not following his advice; otherwise no evil would have befallen him: 'Yet,' said he, 'I cannot leave you here, so lay hold of my tail and hold fast.' Then he pulled him out of the river, and said to him, as he got upon the bank, 'Your brothers have set watch to kill you, if they find you in the kingdom.' So he dressed himself as a poor man, and came secretly to the king's court, and was scarcely within the doors when the horse began to eat, and the bird to sing, and the princess left off weeping. Then he went to the king, and told him all his brothers' roguery; and they were seized and punished, and he had the princess given to him again; and after the king's death he was heir to his kingdom.

A long while after, he went to walk one day in the wood, and the old fox met him, and besought him with tears in his eyes to kill him, and cut off his head and feet. And at last he did so, and in a moment the fox was changed into a man, and turned out to be the brother of the princess, who had been lost a great many many years.

Theme – CCSS RL.2

Theme: _____

Introduction of Theme	**Theme Advancement:**
Details, events, quotes and/or actions in the text that introduce this theme:	New details, events, quotes and/or actions in the text that move this theme forward:

Summary of Theme

_____
_____
_____
_____
_____
_____
_____
_____

Character Analysis (CCSS. RL.3)

In the first box. write how the third son sees himself. In the second box, write how others see him.

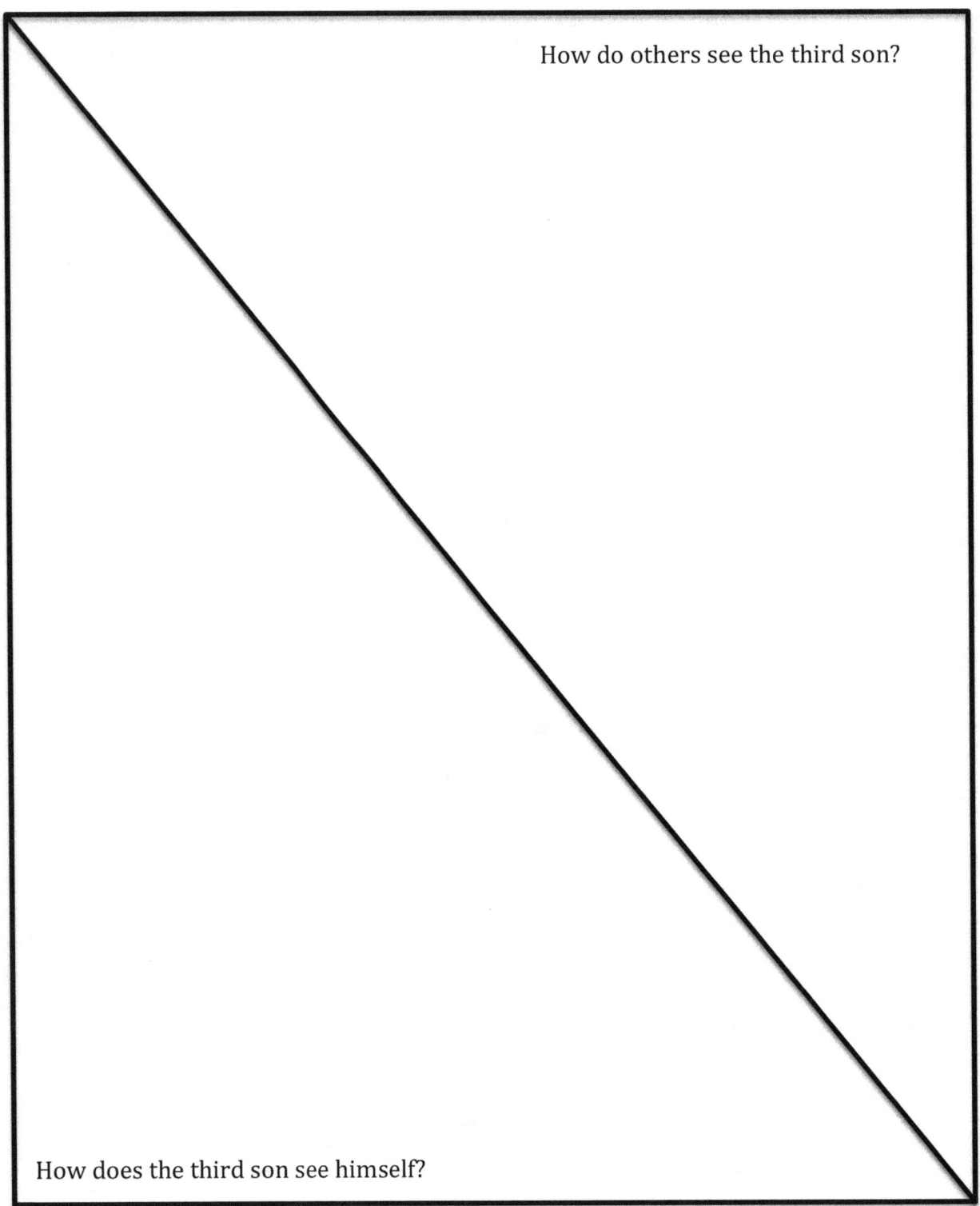

How do others see the third son?

How does the third son see himself?

Author's Choice in Text Structuring

Analyze Choices in Text Structuring (CCSS RL.4 and RL.5)	
1. Sentence Structure: Does the author use shorter or longer or complex sentences or a mixture of all?	
2. Word Choice: Does the author use mostly simple easy to understand words or long formal words?	
3. Tone/Mood: What feeling or mood is created when you read the story. Which specific words contribute to the mood?	
4. Dialogue: Do the characters have a specific vernacular (dialect, slang, regional characteristics)? Is the dialogue believable?	
5. Sensory Detail: Does the author use words that appeal to your five senses? Give examples.	
6. Figurative language: Does the author use words to paint pictures in your mind? What figurative language is used?	

"A long while after, he went to walk one day in the wood, and the old fox met him, and besought him with tears in his eyes to kill him, and cut off his head and feet. And at last he did so, and in a moment the fox was changed into a man, and turned out to be the brother of the princess, who had been lost a great many many years."

Examine and explain the above statement in relation to the theme(s) of *The Golden Bird*.

_____
_____
_____
_____
_____
_____
_____
_____
_____
_____
_____
_____
_____
_____
_____
_____
_____
_____
_____
_____

Summarize the story (CCSS W.4/W.5):

PBL: Choose one of the fairy tales from the Brothers Grimm not in this anthology and rewrite it with a modern flair. For example, you may set it in urban New York or San Francisco, you may choose to write it as a rap, change the characters to famous reality TV stars...whatever you want.

After you re-write your story transform it into a multimedia work. Some examples include: a video starring your friends, a rap album, an illustrated photo album or an ebook. If you choose a scrapbook – remember it has to be multimedia – so snap it into PowerPoint or keynote and set it to music.

Multimedia Presentation Rubric

Student Score	Teacher Score	Appearance
4	4	Good balance of text and graphics. Words are easy to read. Title and headings are easy to distinguish from text.
3	3	Text and graphics are balanced. Words are readable. Titles and headings are distinguishable from text.
2	2	The balance between text and graphics needs some improvement. Some print features distract from readability.
1	1	Poor use of text and graphics. Overall readability is difficult. Poor use of titles and headings.
Score	Score	**Multimedia (graphics, images, music, sound and/or video)**
4	4	Used multimedia components to clarify information and add interest.
3	3	Used multimedia components in presentation.
2	2	Use of multimedia components added little to presentation.
1	1	Use of multimedia components distracted from presentation.
Score	Score	**Content Organization**
4	4	Covers topics completely and in depth. Includes essential information and all components of the original story with modifications for the modern world.
3	3	Includes essential information.
2	2	Includes some essential information.
1	1	Includes little essential information.
Score	Score	**Mechanics**
4	4	All grammar, spelling, punctuation and capitalization are correct.
3	3	1-2 errors in grammar, spelling, punctuation and/or capitalization.
2	2	3-4 errors in grammar, spelling, punctuation and/or capitalization.
1	2	5 or more errors in grammar, spelling, punctuation and/or capitalization.

Teacher Comments: _____

_____

_____

Student Comments: _____

_____

_____

Literary Non-Fiction

Who were the Grimms?

Who? The Brothers Grimm, Jacob and Wilhelm Grimm, were German academics and linguists who collected and published a variety of German folk and fairy tales. The brothers began collecting tales significant to their German heritage around 1807 – in order to promote German nationalism.

Why? During this time, Germany was significantly influenced by France. France occupied the German territory in 1792, and by 1794 they owned the western part of contemporary Germany. France even set up its own legal system and served to transform the German culture. The common trend in intellectual thought at that time was to seek out the neglected German tradition. As intellectuals were trying to recover the respect for German language and culture, at a time when Latin, Greek and French were paramount in academia – the Brothers Grimm sought to revitalize what was once the German academic and cultural landscape. In early 1820s the Prussian state became involved in cultural collections and started funding museums, attributing historical value to items of pre-French era. At the same time, the Brothers Grimm were interested in folktales, another type of cultural artifact. While at university, as students of Professor Friedrich Carl von Savigny, they participated in literary research – which made their love and passion German literature and tales grow stronger.

It was not long before the work of the Brothers Grimm became of great interest for the promotion of German nationalism. By 1822, the brothers published a 3-volume collection of folktales.

The effects of the publication: The Grimm's fairy tales contributed to the national consciousness, as they created a common reading experience among the German people. Children had a sense of belonging to a larger community of readers with similar reading experience and French influences began to slowly fade.

Quick Write: Why where the tales collected by the Brothers Grimm important to Germany?

Hans in Luck

Some men are born to good luck: all they do or try to do comes right—all that falls to them is so much gain—all their geese are swans—all their cards are trumps—toss them which way you will, they will always, like poor puss, alight upon their legs, and only move on so much the faster. The world may very likely not always think of them as they think of themselves, but what care they for the world? what can it know about the matter?

One of these lucky beings was neighbor Hans. Seven long years he had worked hard for his master. At last he said, 'Master, my time is up; I must go home and see my poor mother once more: so pray pay me my wages and let me go.' And the master said, 'You have been a faithful and good servant, Hans, so your pay shall be handsome.' Then he gave him a lump of silver as big as his head.

Hans took out his pocket-handkerchief, put the piece of silver into it, threw it over his shoulder, and jogged off on his road homewards. As he went lazily on, dragging one foot after another, a man came in sight, trotting gaily along on a capital horse. 'Ah!' said Hans aloud, 'what a fine thing it is to ride on horseback! There he sits as easy and happy as if he was at home, in the chair by his fireside; he trips against no stones, saves shoe-leather, and gets on he hardly knows how.' Hans did not speak so softly but the horseman heard it all, and said, 'Well, friend, why do you go on foot then?' 'Ah!' said he, 'I have this load to carry: to be sure it is silver, but it is so heavy that I can't hold up my head, and you

---

CCSS RL: Predict: If it is true that...

Hans in Luck has been described as an ironic fairy tale that inverts the normal "rags to riches" story format – what will happen? Write your thoughts below:

_____
_____
_____
_____
_____
_____
_____
_____
_____
_____
_____
_____
_____
_____
_____
_____
_____
_____
_____
_____
_____

Highlight the most important words in the text and explain why you think they are important. Use evidence from the text to support your conclusions:

Important Words

_____
_____
_____
_____
_____
_____
_____
_____
_____
_____

Evidence Why they Are Important

_____
_____
_____
_____
_____
_____
_____
_____
_____
_____
_____
_____
_____
_____
_____

must know it hurts my shoulder sadly.' 'What do you say of making an exchange?' said the horseman. 'I will give you my horse, and you shall give me the silver; which will save you a great deal of trouble in carrying such a heavy load about with you.' 'With all my heart,' said Hans: 'but as you are so kind to me, I must tell you one thing—you will have a weary task to draw that silver about with you.' However, the horseman got off, took the silver, helped Hans up, gave him the bridle into one hand and the whip into the other, and said, 'When you want to go very fast, smack your lips loudly together, and cry "Jip!"'

Hans was delighted as he sat on the horse, drew himself up, squared his elbows, turned out his toes, cracked his whip, and rode merrily off, one minute whistling a merry tune, and another singing,

'No care and no sorrow,
A fig for the morrow!
We'll laugh and be merry,
Sing neigh down derry!'

After a time he thought he should like to go a little faster, so he smacked his lips and cried 'Jip!' Away went the horse full gallop; and before Hans knew what he was about, he was thrown off, and lay on his back by the roadside. His horse would have ran off, if a shepherd who was coming by, driving a cow, had not stopped it. Hans soon came to himself, and got upon his legs again, sadly vexed, and said to the shepherd, 'This riding is no joke, when a man has the luck to get upon a beast like this that stumbles and flings him off as if it would break his neck. However, I'm off now once for all: I like your cow now a great deal better than this smart beast that played me this trick, and has spoiled my best coat, you see, in this puddle; which, by the by, smells not very like a nosegay. One can walk along at one's leisure behind that cow—keep good company, and have milk, butter, and cheese, every day, into the bargain. What would I give to have such a prize!' 'Well,' said the shepherd, 'if you are so fond of her, I will change my cow for your horse; I like to do good to my neighbors, even though I lose by it myself.' 'Done!' said Hans, merrily. 'What a noble heart that good man has!' thought he. Then the shepherd jumped upon the horse, wished Hans and the cow good morning, and away he rode.

Hans brushed his coat, wiped his face and hands, rested a while, and then drove off his cow quietly, and thought his bargain a very lucky one. 'If I have only a piece of bread (and I certainly shall always be able to get that), I can, whenever I like, eat my butter and cheese with it; and when I am thirsty I can milk my cow and drink the milk: and what can I wish for more?' When he came to an inn, he halted, ate up all his bread, and gave away his last penny for a glass of beer. When he had rested himself he set off again, driving his cow towards his mother's village. But the heat grew greater as soon as noon came on, till at last, as he found himself on a wide heath that would take him more than an hour to cross, he began to be so hot and parched that his tongue clave to the roof of his mouth. 'I can find a cure for this,' thought he; 'now I will milk my cow and quench my thirst': so he tied her to the stump of a tree, and held his leathern cap to milk into; but not a drop was to be had. Who would have thought that this cow, which was to bring him milk and butter and cheese, was all that time utterly dry? Hans had not thought of looking to that.

While he was trying his luck in milking, and managing the matter very clumsily, the uneasy beast began to think him very troublesome; and at last gave him such a kick on the head as knocked him down; and there he lay a long while senseless. Luckily a butcher soon came by, driving a pig in a wheelbarrow. 'What is the matter with you, my man?' said the butcher, as he helped him up. Hans told him what had happened, how he was dry, and wanted to milk his cow, but found the cow was dry too. Then the butcher gave him a flask of ale, saying, 'There, drink and refresh yourself; your cow will give you no milk: don't you see she is an old beast, good for nothing but the slaughter-house?' 'Alas, alas!' said Hans, 'who would have thought it? What a shame to take my horse, and give me only a dry cow! If I kill her, what will she be good for? I hate cow-beef; it is not tender enough for me. If it were a pig now—like that fat gentleman you are driving along at his ease—one could do something with it; it would at any rate make sausages.' 'Well,' said the butcher, 'I don't like to say no, when one is asked to do a kind, neighborly thing. To please you I will change, and give you my fine fat pig for the cow.' 'Heaven reward you for your kindness and self-denial!' said Hans, as he gave the butcher the cow; and taking the pig off the wheelbarrow, drove it away, holding it by the string that was tied to its leg.

So on he jogged, and all seemed now to go right with him: he had met with some misfortunes, to be sure; but he was now well repaid for all. How could it be otherwise with such a travelling companion as he had at last got?

The next man he met was a countryman carrying a fine white goose. The countryman stopped to ask what was o'clock; this led to further chat; and Hans told him all his luck, how he had so many good bargains, and how all the world went gay and smiling with him. The countryman then began to tell his tale, and said he was going to take the goose to a christening. 'Feel,' said he, 'how heavy it is, and yet it is only eight weeks old. Whoever roasts and eats it will find plenty of fat upon it, it has lived so well!' 'You're right,' said Hans, as he weighed it in his hand; 'but if you talk of fat, my pig is no trifle.' Meantime the countryman began to look grave, and shook his head. 'Hark ye!' said he, 'my worthy friend, you seem a good sort of fellow, so I can't help doing you a kind turn. Your pig may get you into a scrape. In the village I just came from, the squire has had a pig stolen out of his sty. I was dreadfully afraid when I saw you that you had got the squire's pig. If you have, and they catch you, it will be a bad job for you. The least they will do will be to throw you into the horse-pond. Can you swim?'

Poor Hans was sadly frightened. 'Good man,' cried he, 'pray get me out of this scrape. I know nothing of where the pig was either bred or born; but he may have been the squire's for aught I can tell: you know this country better than I do, take my pig and give me the goose.' 'I ought to have something into the bargain,' said the countryman; 'give a fat goose for a pig, indeed! 'Tis not everyone would do so much for you as that. However, I will not be hard upon you, as you are in trouble.' Then he took the string in his hand, and drove off the pig by a side path; while Hans went on the way homewards free from care. 'After all,' thought he, 'that chap is pretty well taken in. I don't care whose pig it is, but wherever it came from it has been a very good friend to me. I have much the best of the bargain. First there will be a capital roast; then the fat will find me in goose-grease for six months; and then there are all the beautiful white feathers. I will put them into my pillow, and then I am sure I shall sleep soundly without rocking. How happy my mother will be! Talk of a pig, indeed! Give me a fine fat goose.'

As he came to the next village, he saw a scissor-grinder with his wheel, working and singing,

'O'er hill and o'er dale
So happy I roam,
Work light and live well,
All the world is my home;
Then who so blythe, so merry as I?'

Hans stood looking on for a while, and at last said, 'You must be well off, master grinder! you seem so happy at your work.' 'Yes,' said the other, 'mine is a golden trade; a good grinder never puts his hand into his pocket without finding money in it—but where did you get that beautiful goose?' 'I did not buy it, I gave a pig for it.' 'And where did you get the pig?' 'I gave a cow for it.' 'And the cow?' 'I gave a horse for it.' 'And the horse?' 'I gave a lump of silver as big as my head for it.' 'And the silver?' 'Oh! I worked hard for that seven long years.' 'You have thriven well in the world hitherto,' said the grinder, 'now if you could find money in your pocket whenever you put your hand in it, your fortune would be made.' 'Very true: but how is that to be managed?' 'How? Why, you must turn grinder like myself,' said the other; 'you only want a grindstone; the rest will come of itself. Here is one that is but little the worse for wear: I would not ask more than the value of your goose for it—will you buy?' 'How can you ask?' said Hans; 'I should be the happiest man in the world, if I could have money whenever I put my hand in my pocket: what could I want more? there's the goose.' 'Now,' said the grinder, as he gave him a common rough stone that lay by his side, 'this is a most capital stone; do but work it well enough, and you can make an old nail cut with it.'

Hans took the stone, and went his way with a light heart: his eyes sparkled for joy, and he said to himself, 'Surely I must have been born in a lucky hour; everything I could want or wish for comes of itself. People are so kind; they seem really to think I do them a favour in letting them make me rich, and giving me good bargains.'

Meantime he began to be tired, and hungry too, for he had given away his last penny in his joy at getting the cow.

At last he could go no farther, for the stone tired him sadly: and he dragged himself to the side of a river, that he might take a drink of water, and rest a while. So he laid the stone carefully by his side on the bank: but, as he stooped down to drink, he forgot it, pushed it a little, and down it rolled, plump into the stream.

For a while he watched it sinking in the deep clear water; then sprang up and danced for joy, and again fell upon his knees and thanked Heaven, with tears in his eyes, for its kindness in taking away his only plague, the ugly heavy stone.

'How happy am I!' cried he; 'nobody was ever so lucky as I.' Then up he got with a light heart, free from all his troubles, and walked on till he reached his mother's house, and told her how very easy the road to good luck was.

Really – Literary Devices – (CCSS RL.6)

Culture refers to the cumulative deposit of experience, knowledge, values, attitudes, meanings, roles and even material objects, gathered by a group of people, over generations.

Describe the cultural experience of where you live:

_____
_____
_____
_____
_____
_____

How is the cultural experience of this text different from life in the United States?

_____
_____
_____
_____
_____
_____

Summarize the story:

_____
_____
_____
_____
_____
_____
_____
_____

Happily Ever After

Describe, in detail, how Hans lives **happily ever after**.

Multi-media Comparison: Go to
https://www.youtube.com/watch?v=bddNMy3A6BE

Text   Both   Video

Writing Arguments: CCSS. W.1

Instructions: Write an argument to support the claim that the moral is valid, then transfer your argument to an essay.

Moral: The more or greater your possessions – the greater the burden.

Write an argument to support claim:
Claim 1:
Evidence to Support Claim 1:
Counterclaim:
Evidence to Support Counterclaim:

Critical Non-Fiction – Around the World 1812ish

Between 1812 and 1857, the Brothers Grimm published a collection of folk and fairy tales that grew from 86 to more than 200 stories. In addition to writing and modifying these tales, the brothers wrote collections of well-respected German and Scandinavian mythologies as well. But the stories were not published in isolation. A world of events occurred, both in Germany and globally, in and around 1812 and, in order to fully understand author motivation, it is important to study these events to determine if evidence exists that establishes a source of influence.

Instructions:
Project 1: Use the facts on this page, and any others you find, to write the front page of a U.S. newspaper from any date between 1812 and 1815.

Project 2: After you conduct your research, please use any evidence you find to support influence on the Brothers Grimm and their motivation to publish their collections, as the topic of a formal essay. If you discover no evidence, that is noteworthy as well, and should be supported in your essay.

Around the World 1812ish:

The United States: In 1812, in the United States, James Madison was President and war was declared on the greatest naval power in the world, Great Britain. The conflict, that lasted longer than U.S. involvement in World War I, would have an immense impact on the young country's future. Causes of the war included British attempts to restrict U.S. trade, the Royal Navy's impressment of American seamen, which was a common practice, and America's desire to expand its territory. The United States suffered many costly defeats over the course of the War of 1812, including the capture and burning of the nation's capital, Washington, D.C., in August 1814. Nevertheless, United States' troops were able to spurn British invasions in New York, Baltimore and New Orleans, amassing national confidence and fostering a new spirit of patriotism. The ratification of the Treaty of Ghent on February 17, 1815, ended the war but left many of the most contentious questions unresolved. Still, many in the United States celebrated the War of 1812 as a "second war of independence," beginning an era of partisan agreement and national pride.

Figure 1: Battle of New Orleans.

Little Known Facts:
- Francis Scott Key really did see the "rockets red glare." The missiles used were called Congreves – they looked like bottle rockets – long sticks that spun around in the air.
- "Bombs bursting in air?" Two hundred pound cannonballs!

Germany 1812ish: After Napoleon's final defeat in 1815, the Congress of Vienna met to discuss what was next for Europe. A German confederation was formed to replace the old Holy Roman Empire. It consisted of 38 states charged to balance power and ensure peace and stability after a quarter-century of revolution and war. After months of negotiations and deliberations, the congress established an international political order that was not without its problems.

To read more about the German Confederation:
www.britannica.come/EBchecked/topic/230682/German-Confederation

Fill in the Blanks:

Around the World in 1812ish…

1812: US passed its first foreign aid bill – for Venezuela earthquake relief

1812: Congress authorized war bonds to finance War of 1812

Louisiana admitted as 18th state

1812: Napoleonic Wars

1813:_____

1813:_____

1813:_____

1814:_____

1814:_____

1814:_____

1815: The first 86 African American immigrants, back to Africa, started a settlement in present day Liberia

1815: Maine admitted as 23rd state of the United States

1815: Missouri Compromise passes, allowing Missouri to join the United States despite slavery still being legal there

1815: Spain sells part of Florida for $5 million

Appendix

Rubric

ARGUMENT (9-10)

Description	5 Exceptional	4 Effective	3 Sufficient	2 Minimal	1 Inadequate
Claim: The text introduces a clear, arguable claim that can be supported by reasons and evidence.	The text introduces a compelling claim that is clearly arguable and takes a purposeful position on an issue. The text has a structure and organization that is carefully executed to support the claim.	The text introduces a detailed claim that is clearly arguable and takes an identifiable position on an issue. The text has structure and organization that is aligned with the claim.	The text introduces a claim that is arguable and takes a position. The text has structure and organization that is aligned with the claim.	The text contains an unclear or incomplete claim that poses a vague position. The text attempts a structure and organization to support the position.	The text contains an unidentifiable claim or vague position. The text has inadequate structure and organization.
Development: The text provides sufficient data and evidence to back up the claim as well as a conclusion that supports the argument.	The text provides convincing and relevant evidence to back up the claim and effectively addresses counterclaims. The conclusion supports the claim and evidence.	The text provides sufficient and relevant evidence to back up the claim and addresses counterclaims moderately. The conclusion effectively strengthens the claim and evidence.	The text provides sufficient evidence to back up the claim and addresses counterclaims. The conclusion connects the claim to the evidence.	The text provides evidence that attempts to back up the claim and unclearly addresses counterclaims or lacks counterclaims. The conclusion	The text contains limited evidence related to the claim and counterclaims and/or lacks counter-claims. The text may fail to conclude the argument or position.
Audience: The text anticipates the audience's knowledge level and concerns about the claim. The text addresses the specific audience's needs.	The text reliably addresses the audience's knowledge level and concerns about the claim. The text addresses the specific needs of the audience.	The text predicts the audience's knowledge level and concerns about the claim. The text addresses the particular needs of the audience.	The text considers the audience's knowledge level and concerns about the claim. The text addresses the needs of the audience.	The text illustrates an inconsistent awareness of the audience's knowledge level and needs.	The text lacks an awareness of the audience's knowledge level and needs.
Style and Conventions: The text presents a formal, objective tone that demonstrates standard English conventions of usage and mechanics along with discipline-specific requirements.	The text presents an engaging, formal and objective tone. The text uses standard English conventions of usage and mechanics along with discipline-specific requirements.	The text presents an proper and formal, objective tone. The text demonstrates standard English conventions of usage and mechanics along with discipline specific requirements.	The text presents a formal, objective tone. The text demonstrates standard English conventions of usage and mechanics along with discipline specific requirements.	The text shows a limited awareness of formal tone. The text shows some accuracy in standard English conventions of usage and mechanics.	The text illustrates a limited or inconsistent tone. The text shows inaccuracy in standard English conventions of usage and mechanics.

Rubric for Constructed Response

Score	Description	Score Tally
4	Response answered the question, relates to the reading and student has a grasp of the main story element (s) applicable.	
3	Response answers the question, relates to the reading and student has a grasp of the main story element(s) applicable – but complete sentences were not used and there are problems with spelling and/or grammar.	
2	Response provides a partial answer with limited, incomplete or partially correct information	
1	Response is minimal or vague.	
0	No or incorrect response.	

Teacher Comments: _____

_____

_____

_____

_____

Student Comments: _____

_____

_____

_____

_____

References

Benn, Carl. *The War of 1812.* New York: Routledge, 2003.

Blackbourn, David, (1998).*The Long Nineteenth Century: A History of Germany, 1780-1918.* Wiley-Blackwell.

Grimm's Fairy Tales. University of Pittsburgh. Web. 6 January 2014. <http://www.cs.cmu.edu/~spok/grimmtmp/>

Myint, B. *5 Facts About the Brothers Grimm.* Bio. December 22, 2014. Web. 8 January 2014.

Nipperdey, Thomas. (1996). *Germany from Napoleon to Bismarck: 1800-1866.* Princeton: Princeton University Press.

Primary Documents in American History. Library of Congress. 8 January 2014.

www.ingramcontent.com/pod-product-compliance
Lightning Source LLC
Chambersburg PA
CBHW080943040426
42444CB00015B/3432